GET REAL

4 Steps to Building Generational Wealth Through Real Estate

A Ron's Life Speaks Experience

GET REAL

4 Steps to Building Generational Wealth Through Real Estate

Written by Ron Elliott Jr.
Published by Invisible Clouds LLC

ISBN: 9781731298898

Copyright 2018 Ron Elliott Jr.

All Rights Reserved.

I dedicate this book to my wife and daughters. Real Estate has been a blessing to us and I see the freedom that can be achieved by playing this real life game of monopoly. I pray that you are watching and learning so that you can give the game to your children and their children after them.

"Real estate cannot be lost or stolen, nor can it be carried away. Purchased with common sense, paid for in full, and managed with reasonable care, it is about the safest investment in the world."

Franklin D. Roosevelt

ACKNOWLEDGEMENTS

This is much easier when you write your first book. I of course in all of my doings must acknowledge the Most High. The created can never be great without the Creator. If I had to give one single person credit for my real estate success, It would have to be Mr. Rich Off Real Estate, Brandon Lee. My good brother I thank you for strongly encouraging me to jump into the real estate game. I fought tooth and nail against this movement but you were dedicated to my success. Thank you!

I'd also like to thank Wendy Patton. Wendy you opened my mind to an entirely new and exciting world. I never knew that there were so many possibilities in this world of real estate. You have been essential in my growth as a real estate investor.

I want to acknowledge all of my coaching clients and students that have attended my classes. One becomes a better student by teaching. Thank you for allowing me to grow by sharing my experiences with you. Thank you for challenging me to be a better investor!

TABLE OF CONTENTS

PRELUDE..1

CHAPTER 1

GET YOUR MIND RIGHT 5

CHAPTER 2

GET MONEY..17

CHAPTER 3

GET CREDIT..31

CHAPTER 4

GET REAL ESTATE..55

EPILOGUE 87

LOOKING FOR A SPEAKER?................................91

PRELUDE

"If I knew then, what I knew now…" As a mature adult, this statement is likely to touch your lips from time to time. Life is a cycle. And in the cycle of life, there are patterns that repeat themselves throughout each generation. In the case for most Americans, especially Americans of African descent, one of those patterns is the lack of financial education. We cannot teach what we do not know, right? Have you ever been to the doctor and they ask you for your family history? Do you have diabetes? High blood pressure? Oh, it runs in your family? Do you know why? HABITS! You did not genetically inherit those diseases (unless your diabetes is Type 1). Your habits, specifically the habits that you have inherited from the previous generations, dictated your illness.

GET REAL is a simple, straight to the point guide to get you on the path to developing the habits of the wealthy, and provides you with a few practical methods to begin building generational wealth through real estate. I promise to not overload you, but simply to enlighten and encourage you to put a few simple practices in place that will help you guide the next generation to long-lasting wealth.

Who should read this book? Parents, Grandparents, Teachers, Ministers, Community Leaders, Mentors, and Young People of Working Age. Anyone that has an interest in living in a better, safer, more prosperous community.

I had a conversation with a gentlemen recently. He was of Caucasian persuasion and practiced Orthodox Judaism. He grew up in Brooklyn, New York and was a self-admitted racist. Our conversation was unique because he really wasn't a racist; however, his experiences growing up led him not to trust and to fear people of African descent. "I have been robbed at gunpoint, knifepoint, been beaten badly, and none of the culprits were white!" This was his reason for being a racist. I thought it was a fair assessment. I'm sure there are plenty of Africans in America that feel the same way about their generational oppressor. The gentleman continued, "When I moved here (Michigan), I realized that it wasn't a black thing, it was a location thing. It was a situational thing. Black people here are nice, kind, and working hard to provide for their families. I guess it's about opportunity." His comments led to us speaking about the social economic component of why some minorities engage in criminal activity. We both agreed that if someone is hungry, and you have a steak, if you don't share, you may find yourself on the plate. My point is this: we must share this information and build our community, so that our children and their children can live in a healthy environment without moving away to achieve it.

GET REAL consists of four parts:

1. Get Your Mind Right

2. Get Money

3. Get Credit

4. Get Real

This four-part formula is a simple blueprint for building generational wealth. I hope that you read this material, commit to change, and share this information with as many people as possible.

CHAPTER 1

GET YOUR MIND RIGHT

"Too many people spend money they earned... to buy things they don't want... to impress people they don't like."- Will Rogers

At the age of 26, I was homeless. I'd lost just about everything I owned except for one of my cars, a few clothes, and a few pieces of music recording hardware. I was too ambitious and lacked a proper financial education. I was a college grad and this was not supposed to be my life. I invested all of my money in one thing, got sick, lost my job, weathered the storm by hustling, then found myself in a dangerous situation which led me to walking away from a lot of money. Eventually, things got really tight, I couldn't find a job, and I was stuck sleeping on my friend's couch. This by far was the most humiliating time of my life. I was too bright and too respected to be in this situation. It was like God was previewing Kendrick Lamar's "Humble" with my life, "Sit down, Be Humble!" But it was in this time of my life that I learned how simple life was, and how we didn't need all of the "things" we thought we needed to have peace of mind. In fact, that time proved to be the most peaceful time of my life. I was just grateful to have a roof over my head, food to eat, and clothes to wear.

Growing up, all I saw was "Fly" so all I wanted to be was "Fly". When you were out with me, you could keep your wallet or purse tucked, because I was paying. In one way, I've just always been generous, but in another way, it was the "BOSS" thing to do. My mindset was twisted up. I mean, I grew up with dope boys and poor Blacks elevating to the "Middle Class". Everyone in my community thought that buying a new house, or car, or jewelry, or fur coat, or tv, etc. boosted their status in society. The only conversation we ever had about money was, "save some for a rainy day." And if you live long enough, you'll have plenty of rainy days.

False Profit

I was always a little different, a little more advanced. I was an observer and doer. Prior to graduating high school, I started to notice that buying necklaces, $500 sweaters, and $300 shoes was not the wisest way to use my money. I'd been there, done that, and after visiting college campuses, realized that no one dressed like that in school. I'd been duped. I had spent so much money to impress girls, classmates, and anyone in my presence. That money could have been invested in an index fund that could be paying me big bucks right now. But at the time, I didn't know. As I was educating myself, I realized that entrepreneurship was the best path for me.

I remember sitting at the kitchen table when I boldly proposed to my mother that I should forego college, live at home, get a good factory job, save my money for five years, and start my own business with the money I saved. My mother thought I was crazy and demanded that I attend college. It was so important to her and my family, as it had been their goal since I was a child, for me to become a college graduate. My love and admiration for my mother led to me following her path instead of the path I felt in my heart was right. In this, I failed myself. Many years later, my mother apologized to me. After experiencing the wrath of the city ruining their retirees' pensions, my mother said, "You were right, but I only knew what I knew." You see, we cannot change anything until we change the way we think. When I lost my job, I failed financially because of rebellion. I was taught to save money, but not invest it. Those that I saw saving, had nothing. So I invested all of mine and took a loss. A loss that I almost didn't bounce back from. You don't know what you don't know... but as the poet Pusha T once stated... "If you know... you know!"

MIND ON MY MONEY

Historically, in poorer communities it is almost a sin to discuss money. Money is taught by many to be the "root of all evil". However, this couldn't be further from the truth. Money is a conversation that we should have as soon as we learn to count. Money is a thing. Yes, the love of money, and the desire for the power that it brings can amplify the evil in the hearts of men; but money in itself cannot be good or bad. So how should we view money? We should view money as a tool or as a servant. STOP BEING A SLAVE TO MONEY. MONEY IS YOUR SLAVE.

MINDSET PRINCIPAL #1

STOP BEING A SLAVE TO MONEY. MONEY IS YOUR SLAVE.

This is a principal that the wealthy have mastered. Wealthy people understand the power of LEVERAGE. The biggest use of leverage in American history was slavery. Europeans used the slave labor of Africans to build a country and amass great wealth from the resources of the land. It was the ultimate head start! In today's economy, LABOR is still the most leveraged tool in the playbook for the wealthy. Think about it...you or someone you know has a job. That job pays an hourly wage or salary. However, that wage or salary pales in comparison to the profits made by the primary shareholders of the company. And those shareholders are golfing, sailing their yachts, and spending time with their loved ones while you are at work. Is it fair?

Maybe, maybe not. But it is fact. And now that you know, you can learn to use leverage to your advantage.

MINDSET PRINCIPAL #2

LEVERAGE > LABOR

Leverage is greater than labor! If you want to build generational wealth, you must learn to leverage all of the tools available to you.

Here's a list of things you can leverage right now to begin building wealth.

1. **Time-** We may not all have money, but we all have time. Use it wisely and it can yield great results.

2. **Money-** If you have money, make it work hard for you. Investing is the name of the game.

3. **Intelligence-** You likely have an unique knowledge or skills that others do not. Use your gifts and talents to help you create wealth.

4. **Network-** Maybe you don't have the most time, money, or intelligence, but you know a lot of people and a lot of people know you. Use that to connect people with time, money, and intelligence. And while you're at it... get yourself a piece of the pie.

FIGHT THE POWER

In the late 80s, Public Enemy had a Nation of Millions screaming **Fight The Power** in our Chuck D voices, while wearing Flavor Flav Clocks and African medallions. The fight was for freedom of speech, for freedom from systematic oppression. But there is a greater power oppressing our community. That power is the power of FEAR. In Jay Z's song, "The Story of OJ", Jay has a line that says, "Ya'll still taking advances, me and my team taking real chances..." The deeper meaning behind the line is that his team is winning because they are investing in themselves. Taking a greater risk results in a greater reward. Our community is afraid of failure. And that fear is the most paralyzing fear that we face. Developing the right mindset requires one to overcome fear when it comes to advancing through the ranks. You cannot be afraid to fail and expect to succeed.

One of the best illustrations of why you cannot fear failure is the game of baseball. If you want to hit a homerun, you have to swing for the fences. However, it is unlikely that you will hit a homerun every time at bat. So you swing at the pitches you think you can hit. Sometimes you strike out. But if you never swing, or swing less for the fear of striking out... you'll never hit a homerun. Consider this, in baseball, if you bat a .300, you make BIG MONEY. That's a 30% batting average. That means for every 10 swings you only get three hits. And those three hits might not be homeruns. Those that swing for the fences, those that take real chances make the big bucks. Three hits out of ten can change your life forever. DON'T BE AFRAID TO FAIL.

MINDSET PRINCIPAL #3

STRIKING OUT IS A PART OF THE GAME...SWING FOR THE FENCES!

WHY IS THAT?

When we speak about "Why" or developing our BIG, FAT, STRONG "WHY", we are speaking to our motivation. The only motivation that matters in terms of generational wealth is the next generation. You cannot have a selfish mindset when it comes to applying the knowledge that I am sharing in this book. Yes, I like new things. Yes, I want the big house and the fancy cars. Yes, I want all that I can possess in the realm of prosperity. However, none of those things mean a thing if I cannot position my children and my children's children to live a life of purpose.

Some people are fortunate to experience a life where their purpose and passion align with their pockets. I'm blessed to be compensated to do things that I love to do. This is an awesome feeling. Unfortunately, there is a misconception that this has to be the rule. If you study the Bible, you'll see that the Apostle Paul, who is credited for being the author of a great portion of the New Testament writings, was passionately pursuing his purpose of preaching the Gospel of Yahshua while building tents to provide for himself.

Building generational wealth is a commitment to helping the next generation fulfill their purpose. Imagine what great things you could accomplish in the world if you didn't have to work eight hours a day just to survive. Do not allow your sacrifice to be in vain. Help set your children up so they can avoid the trap of working to live, and allow them a chance to live to work. I am not saying give up on your life's work or abandon your purpose, but set the tempo for those coming after you now. Give them a better platform, a better start. Pass the torch in stride. Let your BIG, FAT, STRONG, "WHY", be the well-being of your children, and their children. In the future, their prosperity will be yours. Your prosperity is bigger than you. It is not just for your benefit, but for the benefit of others in your community and in the future.

MINDSET PRINCIPAL #4

YOUR "WHY" HAS TO BE BIGGER THAN YOU!

CHAPTER 2

GET MONEY

"Money Getter till I'm a 1 Percenter"- Nas

In 1996 I was a senior at the esteemed Cass Technical High School located in Detroit Michigan. At the time, one of the biggest Hip Hop records out was *GET MONEY* by Junior Mafia. Another popular song of that era was "C.R.E.A.M." by Wu Tang Clan. Both songs boasted the same simple message ... GET MONEY. In the movie Scarface, Tony Montana said it like this, "In this country, you gotta make the money first. Then when you get the money, you get the power. Then when you get the power, then you get the women." And the LOX transposed Tony's philosophy into "Money, Power, Respect". Even the good book, the Bible says, "Money Answers All Things". My point is this, if you want to build wealth of any kind, the first thing you have to do is GET MONEY!

There are many ways to get money in this world, but the most common way is good old-fashioned hard work. In today's fast-paced, hyper-entrepreneurial, tech-savvy world, the idea of having a job and working hard to earn a dollar is frowned upon by many. Every day I read or hear successful entrepreneurs speak ill of being employed. And while, I myself, am unemployable, I've never taken the stance that everyone should be an entrepreneur. However, I do strongly believe that it is beneficial to have your money working for you.

In the first chapter, I discussed having money on the mind. If you are becoming more money conscious you are on the right path. However, just thinking about money is not enough. You have to become a Money Getter. A Money Getter is someone that simply knows how to get money. So whether you use your job, your creativity and gifts, your entrepreneurial spirit, or current investments ... you should be doing something to get more money so you can make the money work for you. In this chapter we will discuss the different ways you can get money. Before we dive into each option, let's look at the most important thing you must DO with the money you acquire.

IT'S NOT WHAT YOU GET, IT'S WHAT YOU KEEP

The most common excuse that I hear from people when I speak about advancement is the lack of money. The truth is this, there is not a lack of money in most cases, it is the mismanagement of money. Most people that work, have money that they waste. Some waste it on shoes, others video games, and there are some of us that can't live without our Starbucks every morning. One of the most simple ways to gain access to more money is to cut costs. When you cut costs, you increase your investment power.

Here are 10 Easy Ways to Minimize Your Monthly Expenses:

1. **Unplug Electronic Devices-** Unplugging lights, games, phone chargers, and anything unnecessary while you are

asleep or at work can save you money on your electric bill.

2. **Disconnect the Cable-** Television is overrated. We can just about watch everything we want with cheaper subscription services like Netflix and Amazon. So cut the cord and save big.

3. **Eat at Home-** This is a big one for my family. We have a busy life and it's six of us; so, eating out is a common thing in our household. When we've made a solid effort to eat home cooked meals, we've saved big time and you can too!

4. **Downgrade your Cell Phone-** I know you don't want to hear this, but if your phone is only used for Facebook, Twitter, Instagram, and talking to friends... and it's not making you money, find a lower cost option.

5. **DIY-** This is easy for me, and my wife is pretty great at this as well. I cut my own hair (bald) and that saves me at least $80 per month. My wife does my girls' hair

most of the time herself. What things do you pay for that you can do yourself and save a few dollars?

6. **House Hack-** This is actually a real estate investment strategy that is great for single people. Buy a house with a few friends and split the mortgage.

7. **Transfer Balances-** If you have a card that has a high interest rate, and your credit profile is in a good enough standing to get more credit... get a zero balance card then transfer the balance, and pay your debt off more quickly.

8. **Cancel Your Membership-** If you have a gym membership and never use it... cancel it. If you have one at a fancy club but only use the cardio equipment, cancel it and go to your nearest Planet Fitness.

9. **Give Less-** I have to be honest, this is my least favorite way to cut expenses but sometimes it is necessary. Think about all of the money we spend on holidays alone.

Celebrate a little more modestly now so you can party big later.

10. **Give More-** Give more time to enjoying the simple parts of life. Spend more time in prayer or meditating. Read more. Be Still! This will save you a lot.

All About The Benjamins Baby

Ok, now it is time to get back to the money. I've heard it said that you cannot get rich working a job. I disagree. You can build wealth working a job, it just takes time and wisdom. The cure for this is to invest. Invest in your education. Invest in your skills. Invest in building relationships that will help you move upward in the workforce. Invest in local businesses. Invest in REAL ESTATE! And even if you are just starting at McDonald's, save money to use for investments.

How to Get Money From Your Job

Before you get money from a job, you have to get a job. So let's cover something very basic. One of the highest turnover rates in employment can be found in the service business. If you are unemployed and want to get a job, this is the easiest place to start. The reason being is that you can get hired based on your personality and appearance.

These are things that you can control. These are things that you can work on. Greet people with a smile, listen, be patient, and treat people the way you want to be treated. And finally, be willing to learn. If you go into a service situation with these qualities, you'll find a job. And once you find a job, use it to develop a set of skills that will allow you to grow and seek better opportunities.

Already Working?

If you are already blessed to be in the workforce, you have quite a few options at your disposal. The easiest way is to work a part time business like Uber, Lyft, DoorDash, or Shipt. These types of businesses give you flexibility and can easily be integrated into your life without requiring capital to get started.

Think about your skills, and imagine all of the small businesses that may need your services. Start a part-time business using your unique skills. I pay people to do data entry, make phone calls, answer phone calls, etc. There are many others that do the same. If you have a skill that can be useful in business, take a look at Fiverr.com and Upwork.com. These sites serve as marketplaces for those looking to trade money for services.

If you don't have the stomach for doing your own side hustle, finance someone else's for a return. You have friends that have great ideas and the time to develop them. Why not invest in them? Or, invest a portion of your income into an interest earning account. If your job does matching for your retirement plan, contribute the max every year.

The truth is this, by decreasing your expenses and increasing your income, you are creating the opportunity to gain more money. The end game is to accumulate enough funds to make your money work hard for you so you can work a lot less.

A HUSTLER'S AMBITION

For some, a job is a curse. A job is purgatory and being stuck from 9-5 every day is the lowest form of life. If you dread having a job, you are one of those people crazy enough to create something and willing to suffer until that happens. Entrepreneurs are a different breed of people. The average person isn't built for the uncertainty that comes with taking the leap into the unknown. However, if you are, it can be an exciting and rewarding journey. It also can leave you broken and hopeless. To avoid the latter, let's look at how you can get money to further your investment strength.

Most people think entrepreneurs sit around doing nothing all day. This is one of the biggest myths in society. Yes, if someone builds their business the right way and overcomes the odds of failure, then maybe they have a lot of free time. In my experience, entrepreneurs work harder than anyone else. And that is why it is important to be able to take the profits from business and invest in income-producing opportunities that don't require 80 hours per week.

Building a Business

One of the biggest mistakes I've made in my entrepreneurial career, and I am sure others can attest, is becoming a slave to the business. I grew up during a time when entrepreneurship was not the "it" thing to do. It was difficult to convince people in my community and in my circles to invest in my business. I developed the mindset of having to do everything myself. This was a terrible mindset. It sounds cliché, but teamwork makes the dream work. The power is in having a strong team. And to include a team, you must have a vision and a structure for your business that allows you to focus on the most important part of your business, which is growth.

Your business is a lot like a major league sporting organization and you are the owner. Your goal every year is to win the championship. In your case the championship is not a trophy but a certain level of success as indicated by your desired revenue or profits. You might not achieve this level of success every year; therefore, you spend your time looking for the right pieces to your formula. In a championship sports franchise you have a General Manager, you have Marketing Directors, Administrators, Coaches, Trainers, Public Relations Staff, Star Players, Role Players, Cheerleaders, Fans and more. The owner doesn't play the game or do any of the tasks related to the other positions necessary to run the franchise.

If you want to make more money as an entrepreneur, start by creating a vision for your business and creating a structure that will allow you to grow. Starting out, you may have to play every position. The goal is to replace yourself as quickly as possible.

Raising Capital

Another growth strategy for those in business for themselves is raising capital. The more money you have to invest in your business, the quicker you can build a life outside of your business. Generally, you want to have a solid growth plan and hard numbers to raise capital for your business. Having good credit, a great presentation, and a solid business plan can help set you on the path needed to grow your business and allow you to save for retirement as well as invest in future generations. There are many ways to go about raising money for your business. You can sell ownership or equity in your business. You can borrow money from friends and family. You can use your personal credit to acquire capital for your business or business credit. My goal is not to advise you on financial matters, but to open your mind to the things you can do to increase your income. The more you invest in you and your business, the more likely you are to succeed.

Better Safe Than Sorry

Insurance is a taboo subject in the so called African American community. For many it is an extra bill. For some in the religious community, it is "inviting death" to ever mention having life insurance. Let me be blunt, YOU NEED TO HAVE LIFE INSURANCE. Personally, I like the idea of enjoying the fruits of my labor and building something to leave a legacy for my children and their children after them. Truth is, most people will not invest in themselves nor take the risk necessary to build wealth in their own lifetime. In my opinion, if you will not do anything to build wealth for yourself, you should do something to build wealth for your family. Buying life insurance is the most simple way to build wealth for future generations.

Most people buy auto insurance because it is mandated by law. Feels like a scam until we need it right? Life insurance is optional however. Aside from life insurance, you should also consider disability insurance if you are employed.

You don't have to spend a fortune to be insured. Depending on your health, you can get insurance at a very low rate. So yes, you need to take care of yourself. Your health is your wealth. Death is inescapable. Do your family a favor, buy a life insurance policy today. I am not a financial advisor, so I will not advise you as to how much and where you should you acquire it. I just want to stress the importance of having it. The money that you are able to leave your family can enable them to live a better life. They will be able to carry on where you you left off. So remember, it is better to be safe than sorry.

CHAPTER 3

GET CREDIT

If cash is King, credit is queen! - Ron Elliott Jr.

A FRIENDLY GAME OF CHESS

The main objective in the game of chess is to capture the King. The King is the most important piece but has limited mobility, as it can only move one space at a time. The most powerful piece is the Queen. The Queen has the most flexibility out of all of the pieces and is usually used to protect the King. Cash and Credit are much like the King and Queen in Chess. We use credit to protect our cash. Cash can only move one space at a time, Credit can take us places we couldn't imagine. In this chapter you will learn a lot about credit, how it works, and how to improve your credit so that you can leverage it to build wealth.

Ron's Definition of Credit

The ability to borrow money and to make on-time payments over time.

Let's look at the anatomy of this definition:

- The ability to borrow money, goods or services requires TRUST.

- Making payments on time and over time builds TRUST.

Becoming trustworthy is the most important thing when it comes to unlocking the power of your credit. If you do not remember anything from this chapter, remember this definition and it will guide you in the right direction.

FICO?

Who is FICO? FICO is a company that does predictive analytics. A FICO Score is a predictive analytic based on data provided by the major credit reporting agencies, Experian, Equifax, and Transunion. Your FICO Score is referred to widely as your credit score. FICO scores range from 300 to 850, with the higher number representing less risk to the lender or insurer.

Consumers with excellent FICO scores (usually around 760 or higher, though every lender has different standards) are likely to get the best rates when they borrow, as well as the best discounts on insurance. Your FICO score is your TRUSTWORTHINESS REPORT CARD. Study hard and pass the test!

The 5 C's of Credit

In school a C average is mediocre by academic standards. When it comes to money, mastering these Cs can make you BIG MONEY! Most people acquire credit from banks or financial institutions. These are the most popular methods of acquiring credit. Banks typically look at five things to determine if they will issue credit. These five C's are used to assess the risk of loaning you money. The 5 C's are:

1. Credit History
2. Capacity
3. Collateral
4. Capital

5. Conditions

Let's take a look at each one in detail and learn how they affect our ability to borrow money and make on-time payments over time.

Credit History

Your credit history affects your creditworthiness the most. Your history consists of:

- Payment History
- Total Debt
- Length of Credit History
- New Credit
- Mix of Credit

Payment History

Payment history is the biggest part of your credit score. It accounts for an outstanding 35% of your total score! Payment history on all of your credit accounts span for a period of seven years. So a simple mistake or missed payment can haunt you for a significant amount of time! Your credit report will show what you owe, how much you pay each month, missed payments, and how late the payments are, the more your score will drop! PAY ON TIME, OVER TIME!

Total Debt

Total debt is the second biggest part of your FICO score. Accounting for 30% of your total score, how much you owe is just as important as paying over time. Total debt is also a considering factor when determining your credit capacity. Mortgages and student loans have a low impact in regard to your total debt when it comes to moving the numbers. However, revolving credit like credit cards have a huge impact. Ideally, you want to keep your balances low, even if you have a large amount of credit extended to you.

Length of Credit History

In our definition of credit, "Time" has the most mindshare. ON TIME, OVER TIME! Length of credit determines 15% of your total score. Lenders want to know how long you have had your accounts and if you have paid them on time, over time. An account that you've paid for ten years on time speaks volumes to your ability to make payments. So be faithful in building your credit relationships.

New Credit

Who's that looking in my window? Credit inquiries can't be "blown away" like whoever was looking in Goodie Mob's window. These Peeping Toms account for 10% of your FICO score. Inquiries refer to each application for credit you've submitted in the last two years.

Each inquiry will take five points from your score during the first year unless multiple inquiries were completed for the same product within a few weeks of each other. That just indicates you were rate shopping for a loan or credit card and is typically just treated as a single inquiry.

Credit Mix

Type of credit rounds out the final 10% of your credit score pie. Your credit mix will usually consist of installment loans (house, car), student loans, retail credit or, credit cards. Logic would say that installment loans and student loans being paid on time should work to help your score in a major way and credit cards probably hurt you in a major way if you miss payments.

Capacity

Capacity is all about your ability to carry the debt that you are requesting. Banks only want to lend to those that can comfortably make payments. Your employment history and income are often indicators used to determine this ability. In some cases, the type of income and the stability of the income is considered. Without getting super deep, the bank likely uses what is called a "Debt-to-Income Ratio" to make these determinations. You can calculate your debt-to- income ratio by adding all of your monthly bills and dividing them by your monthly gross income (your income before taxes). The lower your ratio, the better. Ideally, you want to have a ratio around the 30% mark.

Collateral

When it comes to borrowing funds you have two types: secured and unsecured. Secured funds require that you have collateral. Collateral is something you own that you pledge to the lender in the event that you default on the loan. Collateral could be cash, properties, securities, or anything you own of value.

Capital

Your income is considered the primary means of repaying debt. Capital represents your savings, investments, and all other assets that could be used to repay your debt. Capital is often referred to as liquid or non-liquid. Liquidity is determined by how easy the capital can be accessed. Cash is considered more liquid than a house.

Conditions

I look at "conditions" as the bank's contingency plan. Conditions can include the purpose for the loan, economic conditions, or environmental conditions. If the bank doesn't like what you plan to do with the money, they will not lend it. That is why it is hard to get business financing from banks. However, consumer loans are normal and if your numbers are right, you'll likely get the loan you need to buy what you need to buy.

DON'T HATE THE PLAYER, HATE THE GAME

Negative Items

Let's state the obvious; negative items drag your score down. The good news is that the Fair Credit Reporting Act limits the amount of time negative items can be reported. The other good news is that all of your positive items are reported indefinitely. Over time, the impact of the bad stuff diminishes and the newer, more good credit behavior prevail.

Negative items that may appear on your credit report include:

- Charge-Offs
- Collections
- Late Payments
- Bankruptcies
- Foreclosures
- Judgements

- Repossessions
- Tax Liens

Charge Offs

A charge-off occurs when a creditor decides a debt is not collectible. Charge-offs are used as a way to get a debt off of a creditor's books. Removing the debt from their books is solely for accounting purposes. If a creditor writes off a debt it doesn't mean that you are not liable for it, it just means you are extremely delinquent.

By writing off the debt, the creditor's accounts receivables gets a favorable boost but the debt itself is usually sold and hence the barrage of debt collector calls one begins to receive. Debt collection agencies tend to pay pennies on the dollar to acquire uncollectable debt. And that is why most of them are willing to settle a debt with you for half of what you owe or less. It's all profit for them. If you have a charge off on your credit report, it can stay there for up to seven years plus 180 days from the original date of delinquency.

Collections

Collections occur when a debt is severely late. Accounts are usually sold into collections after 180 days of delinquency. Collections is the next step after a debt is charged-off as mentioned above.

So what does a collection do to your credit score? Well, that's tricky. The higher your score, the more it could hurt you. And if it is a small collection, say less than $100, it might not hurt you at all. Sometimes paying them can help, other times it could hurt. Some agencies differentiate between medical collections and non-medical. In my opinion, the safe bet is to avoid going into collections on any debt. It will always hurt you more than it will help you!

Late Payments

Any payment that is more than 30 days late can appear on your credit report. Credit reporting rules do require that after a second payment is missed, all past due payments must be reported.

So DON'T MISS YOUR PAYMENTS! If possible, pay early.

Bankruptcies

Depending on what type of bankruptcy you file, bankruptcies can stay on your credit report for 7 to 10 years from the date filed. Chapter 7 stays on your report for 10 years. Chapter 13 stays on your report for 7 years. I assume this is the case because with Chapter 7 there is usually no repayment of the debt over time.

Foreclosures

Foreclosures are reported for seven years. The good news is that you may not have to wait that long to purchase a new house. You could qualify for a new mortgage in as little as two years.

Judgements

Judgements can remain on your report for up to seven years as well. The term could be shorter is the statute of limitations has expired from the date filed. Check with your state for individual statutes. In my home state of Michigan for debt collection, the statute of limitations is six years.

Repossessions

Repossessions can remain on your credit report for seven years. And it is important to know that even if your property is repossessed, you are still liable for the debt.

Tax Liens

Under federal law, unpaid tax liens may be reported on your credit reports indefinitely. However, the credit bureaus could remove them after a decade or so. Paid tax liens may be reported from the date of payment for up to seven years.

THE FIX

Now that we have an understanding of what credit is and how our scores work, let's work on learning how to repair your credit. On a personal note, I know the stress of having a bogus credit history. At one point in my life, I nearly lost my shirt and my credit suffered tremendously. The primary lesson that I've learned through the process of restoring my credit is that you have to constantly monitor and work on your credit.

However, before you begin fixing your credit, it is important that you create and follow a budget.

Zero-Based Budget

I once attended an event at my first official church home that taught about the importance of money and how it should be used. One aspect of the class focused heavily on getting out of debt. I believe that you should have a plan for your life, and to do that and have a peace of mind, you should have a plan for your money. Zero-Based Budgeting is a method in which one assigns a task to every dollar earned. For example, if your monthly expenses total $2000 and you do your budget and have $200 left over... you have not successfully executed zero-based budgeting. You would still need to give that $200 a job. If you were to allocate that $200 for savings and had $0 left in your budget, then you have successfully completed a zero-based budget.

In my personal opinion, a zero-based budget is the best way to track your expenses and allocate money towards your debt reduction. The formula is simple, [Income-Expenses=Zero]. Expenses include all of your household bills, savings, investments, charitable giving, and debt reduction payments. This method requires work, but it is simple to understand. Let's look a little closer at how this works step-by-step.

1. **Monthly Income-** List all of the money you receive in a month. You can do this on paper, with a spreadsheet, use an app... whatever you like. Include your primary income from your job, your side hustle, alimony, child support, royalty checks, lottery winnings, EVERYTHING.

2. **Monthly Expenses-** List all of your monthly expenses. Be sure to include everything you will pay for in a month. It is a common practice to create categories like, household, vehicle, groceries, spending, debt, utilities, taxes, miscellaneous, to name a few. Even if you do not pay these bills monthly, have a line item expense for them and allocate a portion of your monthly funds to that line item. For example, if you own a home, you may pay your taxes semi-annually. Say your taxes are $6000 per year but you only

make two payments per year. Then you would put $500 away monthly to cover that expense.

3. **Simple Subtraction-** Subtract #2 above from #1 and you should have zero dollars left.

One way to make this super simple is to buy plain white envelopes and write each category on an envelope. Put all of your money in the envelops and pay your bills from those envelopes. Some banks have budgeting applications built into their online platforms. Some of you will not want to have cash on hand and if that is the case, open a couple of different accounts at the bank to make sure that you are staying on track. I suggest something like an account for your income and living expenses, an account for emergency savings, a retirement savings account, an investment account, and spending accounts. If you have a business, you'd follow a similar pattern.

The point that I want to drive home is that if you want to reduce your debt, fix your credit, and position yourself to build wealth through real estate, knowing how much money you have and planning for what you make will only make your life easier and help you to reach your financial goals sooner.

Debt Reduction

I think it is fair to say, most people's primary problem with credit is that they are deeply in debt. Consumer debt is at its highest level according to a recent post by the Washington Post. And most of that debt is credit card debt. The goal is to remove you from the rat race. In order to do this, you have to borrow responsibly. Remember, your credit is your Queen. Love her, cherish her, treat her right and she will feed you.

The debt reduction method that I like the most is the "Snowball Method". The snowball method works the way it sounds. If you created a snowball at the top of a snowy mountain and rolled it down the mountain, it would get bigger and Bigger and BIGGER until it became a GIANT SNOWBALL. This works the same way with your money. Make a list of all your debt (credit cards, car loans, student loans, mortgages, etc.) The goal is to pay off the smallest debt and then apply that payment to the next debt. You continue this path until you have paid off all of your debts.

Dave Ramsey, a well-respected author and authority in finance, recommends that you save $1000 cash for emergencies and allocate whatever money that you are planning to save to eliminating debt. Now to preface this, you will only do this until you are in a healthy position. It is likely that you won't pay off all of your student loans or even your mortgage. But all consumer debt should be eliminated.

Here is an example:

You are able to save $500 per month. You have three credit cards with the following balances: $1000, $5000, $7500. You have minimum payments of $27, $99, and $171. You make all of your payments on time. First you will save $500 for two months to create your emergency savings. If you ever have to use this money, you will pause your plan and replenish that savings. In the third month, you will pay $527 on your $1000 card. This card will of course have interest so each month the balance on all cards increase. Month four, you likely would have paid the smallest card completely off depending on the interest rate. Once that card is paid, you will take the $527 and add it to the $99 card monthly until it is paid off. Then you'd add the $628 payment to the $171 until all of the cards are paid off.

Once you have gotten rid of the dead weight, you can then return to saving and investing your money. I recommend working towards one year of living expenses. It may take a little while to get there, but when you unlock the power of real estate investing, that time can be shortened drastically.

Getting Your Hands Dirty

You are on your way to building generational wealth. The only problem is that your credit isn't what you want or need it to be to begin taking advantage of all that real estate has to offer. No worries, with a little bit of work, we can get that credit score right where it needs to be. Let's get our hands dirty and FIX OUR CREDIT!

I've discussed debt reduction. But maybe that isn't your problem. So let's look at the steps everyone should take to improve their credit score.

Step One- Get Your Report

I was having a conversation with a friend that wants to sell his house and buy a new one. One of the first things I asked was, "How's your credit?" His response, "I don't know". Here's the thing, if you are not keeping track of your credit, you won't know what your next move should be. Pull your credit report today. There are many services online that will give you a free annual report. AnnualCreditReport.com is one of those sites. Your bank may offer a similar service and if you ever have your credit pulled for a car or credit card, you can request a copy of your report. You want to get your report from all three credit bureaus: **Experian**, **Equifax**, and **Transunion**.

Step Two- Get Your Fine Tooth Comb (Review It)

Check your report for accuracy. Make sure you examine all three reports in depth. Make sure your name is correct, address is correct, social security number is correct. Check every account.

If you see an account on your report that you did not open, highlight it. If your balances do not match your personal records, make a note. Look for negative items like those mentioned earlier in the chapter. If those exist, we will want to work to have them resolved or removed.

Step Three- Move… Get Out The Way!
(Dispute and Remove)

If you find anything on your credit report that is inaccurate, past the statute of limitations, misleading, incomplete, or questionable, you can request to have that information removed.

Requesting removal is as simple as mailing each credit reporting agency a letter by certified mail. Each agency has a method by which they prefer you do this. I recommend visiting their websites to learn the best way.

If you don't want to bother with any of this, I recommend going to ronslifespeaks.com/credit and I'll refer you to a credit repair service.

Once you mail the letter, the credit bureau has 30 days to respond. If you ordered your report online from somewhere like annualcreditreport.com they get an additional 14 days to respond. You may do this entire process online, but based on personal experience, it is not that effective. Mail is the way to go with this one.

When you write your letters, be sure to include all of your information as well as everything you are disputing in detail. It is the credit bureaus responsibility to provide proof. If you have supporting documents for your case, by all means supply them. This is a process, so be patient, and persistent. When you make a dispute, by law they have to investigate. Don't wait, get to disputing!

A QUICK NOTE- If you have an old debt on your report that will come off of your report soon, you may not want to dispute it, if so you may restart the clock. So keep that in mind.

GET A BOOST

Remember your credit score is weighted. You may not have any negative items on your report, no collections, and pay your bills on time and still have a lower score. Why? Debt utilization. Remember, your debt-to-credit ratio accounts for 30% of your FICO Score. Here are a few tips and tricks to make sure you keep your ratio in the right range.

1. The most obvious way is debt reduction, as we've already discussed.

2. Request a limit increase. This will lower your credit utilization.

3. Become an authorized user. This will also give your more credit and lower your credit utilization.

4. Consolidate your credit cards with a loan or 0% Interest card. This will allow you to have a lower rate and to pay your debt off quicker. Also installment loans are looked upon more favorably than revolving credit.

5. Get a secured loan from your credit union. I've used this trick very effectively. You take out a loan secured by your money. Pay on it monthly and when it is paid off, the credit union reports it on our credit. Great way to build credit.

YOUR HEALTH IS YOUR WEALTH

Taking care of your credit is a cornerstone to your financial health. If you want to build generational wealth, you need your finances to be Herculean in nature. The best way to remain financially healthy is to stick to your budget, pay your bills on time, constantly monitor your credit, and make fixes a needed. In doing this, you will protect your King (Cash) and be able to use your Queen (Credit) to capture the prize!

CHAPTER 4

GET REAL ESTATE

"Ninety percent of all millionaires become so through owning real estate. More money has been made in real estate than in all industrial investments combined. The wise young man or wage earner of today invests his money in real estate." -- Andrew Carnegie, billionaire industrialist

There is a great deal of truth to Mark Twain's famous quote, "Buy land, they aren't making any more of it." We live in a world of cryptocurrency, paper currency, credit, and debit cards. All of these things change and can change how we track the services that we provide. Humans decide the value of the currency. However, necessity determines the value of the things we need to survive. We need water, we need food, we need clothing, we need energy, and we need shelter. In business, the people that satisfy our human needs, tend to make good, consistent money. The good news is that you can join them.

In my personal experience as an entrepreneur, real estate is the great equalizer in terms of the average person being able to compete economically with the big boys. In this chapter you will not learn everything you need to become a professional real estate investor. That takes time, practice, and a lot of studying. What you will learn, however, are the building blocks or the fundamentals, as I like to call them, to help you on your journey to building generational wealth through the buying and selling of real estate.

In this chapter I will cover the following topics:

- Why Real Estate?- Why use Real Estate as your wealth building tool.

- Why Now?- Why you should start right now and not wait for perfect conditions.

- How to Think About Real Estate- Mindset is a Must!

- Building your Real Estate Team- Real Estate is a contact sport, you'll need support.

- The Two Main Types of Real Estate Investing- We'll discuss the game as a whole.

- The Best Strategies for Building Long-Term Wealth- You have to have a plan.

- Exit Strategies- Knowing when to hold 'em and when to fold 'em is key.

Again, one book will not make you an expert. So read as many books and attend as many classes as possible. YouTube is a great resource as well joining local real estate clubs and groups. Ok, now let's dig in and start building GENERATIONAL WEALTH!

WHY REAL ESTATE? WHY NOW?

I have a very wealthy and respected mentor, and one of the key life principles he follows is "Keep it

Super Simple" or KISS for short. The most simple answer as to why one should invest in real estate is that people will always need somewhere to live. Aside from the super simple reason to invest in real estate, there are many financial reasons that one should become a real estate investor. Why now? There is no better time than the present. Here are a few good reasons to own real estate.

- Appreciation
- Cash Flow
- Leverage
- Tax Savings

Wealth Generation

A penny saved is a penny earned right? Real estate has the power to save you a penny and earn you two. Let's learn about the different ways to build wealth through real estate. **Appreciation, cash flow, leverage, and tax savings** are all mechanisms that help real estate investors build massive wealth. The good thing is that anyone can do this. So make sure you understand the following principles as they will lead you on the path to generational wealth.

Appreciation

When I was a child, I was a huge Star Wars fan. I'm grown and I'm still a huge Star Wars fan! My mother was gracious enough to buy me all of the Star Wars toys at the height of the franchise's success. I had the original Millennium Falcon (The big one). One day all of my toys disappeared. I never really thought about my toys until one day in 1999. When Star Wars introduced Episode 1 in 1999 I was super excited. While the movie left a little bit to be desired, there was an amazing spectacle in the lobby of the theater that caught my eye. I saw a gentleman selling the same exact Millennium Falcon that disappeared from my toy vault for $1000. All I could think about was how I could have been selling my Millennium Falcon. Unlike most toys, the Millennium Falcon had appreciated over time.

Keeping it SUPER SIMPLE… appreciation is an increase in the value of an asset over time. Classic cars appreciate, art appreciates, classic toys appreciate, and real estate appreciates among other things. When discussing real estate, there are two types of appreciation: natural appreciation and **forced appreciation.**

Natural Appreciation

Natural Appreciation is influenced by the market. Things like inflation or the simple economic principles of supply and demand. In fact, as of the writing of this book, my local market has been experiencing a tremendous leap in natural appreciation... which will eventually become depreciation as the supply gets greater and the homes are no longer so scarce.

Forced Appreciation

Forced Appreciation is pretty cool because it is a value add kind of thing. Forced appreciation occurs when you make something better. So when you add a bedroom or a bathroom to the house, the value will increase.

Appreciation, whether natural or forced, is a great thing. But to rely solely on appreciation to build wealth would be foolish. It is important that while you are on this path to trust the numbers and not your emotions. Appreciation can give you a false sense of success. Be mindful that it is mostly controlled by market conditions.

Cash Flow

Cash Flow is the incoming and outgoing of cash in a business. Real estate investing done properly should yield a positive cash flow. And a positive cash flow provides a steady stream of income. Multiply that income by various properties and one can replace their income, pay off debts more quickly, or invest in more income producing opportunities.

A brief warning about cash flow. Buying a few rentals and getting them to a positive cash flow is not a reason to quit your job. In order to build a cash flow big enough to replace your income, you'd need a massive amount of "doors" or places that you collect rent. So in my opinion, the best use of any positive cash flow that you are getting is to put it back into your business.

Leverage

How do you move a boulder without Superman? Leverage! What is leverage? Leverage is borrowed capital or money used to increase the potential return on an investment. Most people cannot afford to pay $100,000 cash for a property. Leverage allows us to pay $20,000 to acquire that $100,000 property.

Once the property is acquired either through bank financing or private financing, the sole mission becomes paying down the loan. Paying down the loan builds equity and equity is what translate into wealth. As previously mentioned, this is where cash flow becomes beneficial. Paying down your loans quickly will help you increase your profits when you sell.

Tax Savings

While owning properties create more tax liabilities, they also provide a few tax benefits. Owning rental properties is a business. All businesses allow the owners to write off certain expenses.

The tax benefits of real estate include depreciation, FICA or Payroll taxes, appreciation, capital gains tax savings, **IRA tax free investing** and more. I strongly encourage you to hire a tax professional that invests in real estate or works with a lot of real estate investors.

Building wealth through these four factors takes time and experience, but they are definitely attainable. How these factors affect your investing career will mainly come down to what type of strategy you decide to employ. When one is flipping houses, appreciation and leverage come into play the most. There may be some tax savings from a business standpoint, but there is definitely no cash flow. In taking a long-term buy and hold approach, a savvy investor is able to maximize each factor as they build wealth.

"WE SUPPOSED TO BE HERE!" (INVESTOR MINDSET)

You couldn't get me to even think about real estate a few years ago. In my mind, you needed a lot of start-up capital to even consider investing in real estate. And honestly, it looked like much harder work than what I was currently doing that I couldn't wrap my mind around it. I was suffering from a condition called "Stinking Thinking". I was so uneducated about real estate that I was missing out on the golden goose. Once I became educated about the game, I became obsessed with it.

Real estate investing to me is like the lovechild of music and Monopoly. Real estate allows you to be creative in solving complex issues, but it follows simple rules like a board game. As you transition into becoming a real estate investor, I think it is very important that you adopt this view point. Being too rigid will hurt your business. Not playing by the simple rules will break your pockets! A great real estate investor is always looking for opportunity. A great real estate investor knows their numbers and sticks to their criteria.

Up to this point if you believe that real estate is too hard or that you don't have enough money... you are wrong. I have started several businesses over the years and real estate has been the most straightforward and the most profitable within the first six months of starting. It is my hope that you make up your mind to use real estate as a way to build wealth for you and your family. Real estate should not be your only means of doing so, but it definitely should be a viable option.

Now that you are certain that you should be investing in real estate, it is important that I encourage you to become educated about real estate before throwing all of your eggs in the basket. One of the most dangerous things you can do with your money is invest without doing any type of research. This book is intended to give you a launching pad but it doesn't cover all of the ins and outs of investing. Don't look at real estate as a means to get rich quick. Dip your feet in the water, check the temperature, and ease into the game. Take your time, do it right, think long-term. Building a massive amount of wealth will require you to be able to swim amongst sharks. So if you are going to dive into anything, dive into education. If time is an issue, and money is not, find a professional that is willing use you as a private lender. We use private lenders to buy properties and pay our lenders a high rate of return secured by real estate. Again, make sure that you are properly educated before making any moves in this business.

"THIS THE WAY PLAYERS PLAY" (TEAM SPORT)

"Just the way players play, all day, every day, I don't know what else to say!" - Notorious B.I.G.

Real estate is a team sport. And with any team sport, you want to make sure that you build a winning team with great chemistry in order to win games. When putting together your team, you want to work with people that do what they do full-time. You want to work with people that are fully committed to the role they play.

If you have a family, your team starts at home. As of this writing, I am going on fourteen years of marriage. My wife is the first and most important member of my team. As a full-time entrepreneur, I have no stability. There are no sick days, no off days, no matching retirement plan, nothing. I have none of the comforts of an employee and all of the worries of a business owner. However, my wife works full-time, has health benefits, a retirement fund, and can take a day off of work if the kids need to go to the doctor. More importantly than all of those things, my wife supports my vision. She's my number one cheerleader. If you are going to be successful in anything in life, you are going to need someone else to champion your cause. So if you have a significant other or close family members that you engage with, make sure they are on your team and want you to win. If not, you may need to move a few players out your rotation. DON'T GET RID OF YOUR SPOUSE! I know how some of you think. If your significant other isn't down for the cause, put your head down and put your plan to work. When they see the benefits of your work, they'll come around. Sometimes the people that believe the least are the people closest to you.

When I first started on this path, my wife had no clue what I was talking about! She could not understand how I was going to make money without spending all of our money. She didn't understand why I didn't sue this person or that person when a deal went sideways. She had no clue. One thing that I did to help her understand my world was to take her to a real estate training with me. Once she left, she saw the vision and knew it was real and not just me saying, "We're going to get rich!" The moral of the story is this, stay dedicated, get educated, and make sure your loved ones are educated as well.

The other players on your team will include:

- Mentor
- Lawyer
- Accountant and Bookkeeper
- Real Estate Agent
- Insurance Agent
- Lenders
- Contractors & Handymen
- Property Manager

Let's talk about each person's role on your team.

Mentor

When I was a kid my father dropped a very important jewel on me, he said, "Son, learn from other people's mistakes." He was speaking in terms of his life and where he went wrong. I took what he said to heart and have not made the same mistakes he has made. He told me that if I see someone burn their hand on the stove, there is no need to put my hand in the fire to see if it is hot. The same goes with finding a mentor. I believe a mentor is the most important person on your team outside of your spouse or significant other. I did a million dollars in real estate deals within my first six months of taking investing serious. I can attribute 80% of that success to having strong mentors and the other 20% to taking action. You will learn the most from people that are doing what you want to do. You can share in their successes and failures.

If you are like most people, you are probably spinning your wheels trying to figure out where you would find such a person that is willing to share all of their secrets of the ooze. In my opinion, mentors are earned. Before I had mentors that I could touch and speak with on a regular basis, I had "mentors in my mind". A "mentor in my mind" would be an expert that has written a book about whatever I was interested in learning. Over time, I'd amassed a great amount of wisdom from studying the philosophies of great business people willing to share their knowledge and wisdom through words.

Once I made myself more attractive through self-education, other successful people drew to me. And I being a student made sure to humble myself and learned from them. Then the magic began to occur! See, when successful people see you working hard and seeking knowledge from them, the more they share. The reason behind it is that success comes from giving. Most of us miss this point. We focus on what we "want" more than what we can "give." However, successful mentors succeed more by giving away knowledge. The more they share, the more they succeed. You must also understand that successful people are not willing to invest their time into people that are not putting forth their best effort. Mentors want to share in your victories!

A great example of this is my real estate mentors. My mentors are two totally different types of investors and personalities. Both are tenacious business people but they use very different strategies. The one thing they have in common is that they take every chance they can to gloat about my success. They love to talk about how they helped me close a deal. I never mind because it is true and it lends credibility to my business.

My point to you is this, a strong mentor will help you win much faster than you will on your own. And if you start on your own, follow someone online, or an author, or anyone that is doing what you want to do as closely as possible.

Bottom line, find you a mentor to help guide your journey. They will save you a lot of stress and will be able to connect you to the other members on your team.

Lawyer

Love them or hate them, a good lawyer can help you succeed in all aspects of life. The best way to find a lawyer is to ask for referrals from other real estate investors. You can meet investors through various meetups that likely happen in your local area. Ask for recommendations. You may need more than one as some lawyers specialize in certain areas of real estate. Your lawyer will mostly draft and review documents for you or set up your business entities. In the event that you get sued, and it can happen, you'll want to have someone that knows what they are doing on your side. If you cannot afford an attorney to start out, sign up for Legal Shield. You can go online and find contracts and other documents needed to do business. Once you find them online, modify them for your state then have your legal shield attorney review the docs. This is not the most ideal situation, but it can help you get started. As you advance as an investor, you'll be able to do a lot of the paperwork yourself and having your lawyer review rather than draft will save you a ton of money!

Accountant and Bookkeeper

If you are planning on building a viable real estate investment portfolio, you will want to have both a skilled bookkeeper that works with real estate investors as well as a Certified Public Accountant (CPA). Ideally, these two professionals will have real estate in their investment portfolios as well. Your bookkeeper will help you stay organized throughout the year and your CPA will work to help you take advantage of the tax strategies beneficial to real estate investors. In fact, make sure that you always have a great mentor, lawyer, CPA, and bookkeeper for any business that you engage in.

Real Estate Agent

It only makes sense that if you are running a real estate business that you should employ a real estate agent to help you grow your business. Real estate agents are great for researching the market, finding hot deals, and helping you sell the properties that you have acquired when you are ready to cash out. When looking for an agent, you want someone that is hungry. A hungry agent is going to work hard for you. A more seasoned agent may be beneficial if you are working more sophisticated deals. Either way, having an agent on your team is always a good idea, especially if you are planning to invest passively.

Insurance Agent

Landlords must have insurance to protect their properties. You want to make sure that you build a good relationship with companies that insure rentals. Brokers are probably best because they can help you shop around, but if you find an individual agent that has your best interest at hand, keep them around.

Lenders

Lenders are a critical piece to every real estate investor's business. Lenders allow us to have leverage and build our real estate empires. When seeking lenders, you want to shop for the best rates for your situation. And just like every member on your team, you will need to cultivate a great relationship with your lender. Whether you borrow from a national bank, credit union, mortgage broker, or private lender, you will need money and a lender will be your best friend in this business!

Contractors & Handymen

To achieve success in any business you will need a solid network. This cannot be more true than when dealing with contractors and handymen. There is never enough people available to get things renovated, fixed, or replaced, especially when the market is hot. You will want to ask for referrals when hiring people to do work. And I would suggest getting multiple bids. Some things will require a contractor and others a handyman. Aside from referrals, go to Home Depot and network. There are contractors and handymen coming and going all day at Home Depot.

As a word of advice, never pay everything upfront when dealing with a contractor or handyman. You may find yourself in a situation where the work you need done is only partially completed and you have to find a new person to finish it. I'm speaking from personal experience. I hired a handyman to do some work for one of my properties and he didn't finish the work. I never pay in advance for this reason. Later he called attempting to collect his money, and my response was simply, "I'll pay you the rest of your money, when you finish the rest of my job!"

Property Manager

The final member of your team will save you the day-to-day stress of running a rental business. Your property manager will put new tenants in your property, make sure things get fixed, collect rent and handle evictions. A good property manager will help you sleep at night for a small percentage of the revenues that your property generates. I am a big proponent of being as hands off as possible in your investments. You are not looking for another job, you are looking for a way to make your money, make money!

A strong team will definitely help you to achieve your goals more quickly than attempting to take this journey alone. You may not need every member at every step of your business, but if you intend on building generational wealth through active investing, you'll use each and every member.

TYPE 2 (THIS IS NOT DIABETES)

There are many ways to make money in real estate. Each method that may come to mind likely falls into one of two categories; Buy and Sell or Buy and Hold. These are the two strategies that cover the gambit of investment techniques and tactics used by real estate investors worldwide. Let's take a look at each strategy more in detail.

Buy and Sell

Buying and selling real estate is a job! If you want to make large sums of money in a short period of time, buying and selling may be the way to go. Using a buy and sell strategy is good for one reason and one reason only, to build your capital. Most people get excited about flipping a house but have no clue what it takes and how things can go terribly wrong, terribly fast. It is a risk reward type of situation. The greater the risk, the greater the reward. And while overall, this strategy is less risky than holding properties, it doesn't allow you to take advantage of the taxes.

A buy and sell strategy will not allow you to be passive about real estate. Assuming a "Fix and

Flip" approach will require you to learn several skills to ensure your success. You will need to know how to market, how to negotiate, how to estimate repairs, and have the capital necessary to float expenses and unexpected problems. However, if you have what it takes, this strategy can work very well and help you to make larger sums of money than just buying and holding real estate.

When you hear the commercials about flipping real estate with no money out of your pocket, this is the strategy that is being used. And while you can do real estate with other people's money, it is much more challenging than you think. I've been very successful at doing real estate deals with other people's money. You can learn the same strategy I used to make Big Money at ronslifespeaks.com/courses. One thing you will learn about this business is that you will either win because you have financing in place or because you are extremely creative. If you have both, you can rule the world.

In terms of building generational wealth through real estate, this strategy doesn't necessarily apply. I believe that it is smart for a real estate investor to flip a few houses a year if possible as it will help you make more money than just buying homes and renting them. But if you want to build transferrable wealth, you will want to take a more stable approach.

Buy and Hold

Buying and holding real estate is definitely one of the best ways to build generational wealth. This strategy allows you to take advantage of cash flow, leverage, appreciation, and taxation. Real estate in general appreciates over time and while there are fluctuations in the market, if you use this strategy for long-term wealth those fluctuations should not hinder your overall goal. Always remember that there is only so much land and so much shelter available. And shelter is a need that will never go away.

Using "buy and hold" as a long-term growth strategy will take time and patience. If done correctly, buying and holding should yield you a continuous cash flow. That continuous stream of income can be used to pay down debt and increase your equity in the properties that you acquire over the years.

As with everything there are pros and cons to buying and holding real estate.

The pros are all of things that I've mentioned earlier in the book:

- Appreciation
- Leverage and Loan Pay Down
- Cash Flow
- Tax Breaks

The cons are:

- Market Conditions
- Legal Issues
- Slow Appreciation
- Management Issues

Market Conditions

When you hold onto a property the value will go up and the property will go down. If you buy the property the right way, it may not matter. But market conditions can affect tenant relations as well. If the market drops dramatically, there may be an increase of buyers vs. renters. And if for some reason you need to sell your property during a down market, you could potentially take a loss. But market conditions will have less of an impact if your plan is longer term. Most people that amass great wealth from business use real estate to hedge against losses in the stock market. So don't let market conditions scare you. Use the market conditions as an indicator as to when to buy and when to sell.

Legal Issues

Legal issues will arise in any business endeavor if you participate long enough. When renting properties you will surely run into tenant issues from time to time. There will be times where you will have disputes with the local government concerning your property. These things just come with the territory. That's why you'll have a great lawyer on your team!

Slow Appreciation

I do not want you to get confused about this appreciation thing. Slow appreciation is still appreciation. In terms of natural appreciation, the property will appreciate and depreciate over time because you are holding it. If you were to rehab and sell, then you benefit greatly from forced appreciation. So while this is a con, you should not base your decision to invest in a property on the potential to appreciate.

Management Issues

Management issues really only come into play if you manage your properties yourself. I strongly encourage you to hire a property manager to deal with the day-to-day issues of collecting rent, scheduling repairs, or evicting and placing tenants. I want you to invest in real estate, not work in real estate. Investing in real estate means working on growing your portfolio, not doing the day-to-day ground work to manage your properties.

Wealth Building Game Plan

I was recently invited to participate as a panelist at a real estate investment seminar. At the end of the discussion each panelist was asked to give one piece of advice to the audience. My advice was simply this, "Start!" This book is not the "end all, be all" of investing. In fact, this book is only an introduction. I hope that you take this information and use it to seek more knowledge. I want you to use the knowledge that you are acquiring to build wealth for you and your family.

So let's explore a few options to get us started on building generational wealth!

The first thing you will have to do is determine how much money you need to provide you the economic freedom to live the life you want and to give the next generation a solid launch pad to do the same. Once you've figured out that number, you will need to think about how you get there. Don't worry if it seems out of reach. It is possible that it may take two generations to achieve this goal. But what if it took three? So what! The point is to develop the mindset of building wealth with each generation.

Now that we know what we need to have to achieve our goals, the next and easiest thing to do is to get insured. Once you have insured yourself, it is time to start making more money! You'll need money to engage in real estate successfully. If you don't have a lot of money, get with your family and pool your money together. Do whatever you have to do to get in the game.

While you are getting your money together, work on your credit. You do not need credit to begin investing because you can partner with someone that has good credit. But you want to improve your chances to do every type of deal possible. Now let's take a look at a sample plan.

Sample Real Estate Investing Plan 1

This plan is based upon acquiring properties with a down payment and decent credit.

Purchase a multi-unit home (duplex, triplex, quad) if possible, live in a unit and rent the other unit(s). This is a great way to start for single individuals or couples without children. I'd hire a property manager to remain a bit anonymous when dealing with tenants. Using this plan will allow you to live rent free as you allow your other unit(s) to pay down your mortgage. Use the money that you would use to pay a mortgage or rent to save for the down payment on your next property.

Do your best to buy another multi-unit. Once you have three or four multi-units, consider using the profits to pay off the first home, then the second, third, etc. Hopefully, these properties will have appreciated and you can use the increased cash flow to purchase more properties or sell them to acquire a larger property like an apartment complex. The goal would be to do this over and over until you build a nice portfolio of apartments or just multiple doors in general.

In terms of numbers, theoretically, if you owned three quads free and clear, you should be able to make somewhere between 8K-10K per month. That doesn't sound like a lot of money, but if that is coming in as a residual income while you are able to work... in ten years, you should have a million dollars. So it doesn't take a lot, it just takes discipline.

Sample Real Estate Investing Plan 2

This plan is for the hands-off investor. If you want to make your money make money and you not lift a finger, consider becoming a private money lender. This plan is for people with money in a retirement plan or those that have money tied up in CDs or a dormant savings account without any interest.

Active investors like myself partner with passive investors to flip properties and we pay generous rates of return. You may know an investor that is skilled at real estate already and can use your money to continue to fund their business. All active investors need capital to acquire new properties. If you'd like to learn more about this, visit http://ronslifespeaks.com/private-lending.

There are other ways and combination of ways that you can build wealth with real estate. There are real estate funds that are traded on the market, there are turnkey rentals where you buy properties with renters already present. You can buy notes, fix and flip, owner finance long-term investments, or you can do nothing! The choice is yours! I pray that you choose wisely.

EPILOGUE

"A man that has not prepared his children for his death has failed as a father!" -T'Chaka (from Black Panther- The movie)

When we are young we live for ourselves. We live for our pleasures, for our desires. We run from our fears until we are forced to face them. When we mature, we realize that we are not just responsible for ourselves, but for our family and our community. And with that responsibility comes the obligation to share knowledge and resources.

When I was a young man attempting to build an empire, I was shunned by just about everyone. No one could see past a job, everyone was afraid of failure. I've watched many people of various backgrounds prosper from the same thoughts and ideas that I possessed and the reason being is that they had a community behind them. When they showed an interest in computers, their parents provided them with computers. Those that won were not discouraged by their community but empowered. In sharing this information I am fulfilling my obligation to my community.

This book alone is not enough to make you Warren Buffet or Mansa Musa. I hope it is enough to make you think about your mindset, your money, your credit, and take action on implementing real estate investing into your wealth generation plan. And if you don't have a solid plan for generating wealth, to inspire you to create one.

Real estate has been very good to me thus far and I expect it to only get better. Don't get discouraged if you begin and fail. Don't be discouraged when the market drops. Continue to educate yourself about economics and markets, and save money to invest with when the markets are down. Become a professional learner and doer. Take action. Consistent action with error will help you more than watching from the sideline. Just be sure to make the necessary adjustments to your plans to ensure long-term success. AND... BE DEDICATED TO TEACHING THIS INFORMATION TO THE NEXT GENERATION!

I wish you much success!

Coach Ron

LOOKING FOR A SPEAKER?

GENERATIONAL WEALTH EVANGELIST...master motivator, author, speaker and coach... Ron is the Professor X of inspiration helping audiences and clients to **Discover the SUPERHERO Within** and **Let Their Lives Speak Volumes**.

Ron's unique blend of relatable stories, unfiltered truth, wisdom, and natural humor makes for a fun and enlightening experience. A former college educated drug dealer, Ron has gone from homelessness to inspiring thousands of people through his books, coaching, and seminars.

Ron has the ability to speak on many topics including:

- Purpose
- Family Finance

- Marriage
- Spirituality
- Basketball
- Music
- Youth
- Real Estate
- Fitness
- Entrepreneurship
- Personal Development
- Business Development

Looking to book your next speaker? Want someone that is engaging and entertaining? Book Ron at:<u>ronslifespeaks.com/book-ron</u>

Want to Learn More About Real Estate?

Ron has a few online classes about real estate. You can check them out at: ronslifespeaks.com/courses

Need Coaching?

Ron has personal development and real estate coaching programs available at: ronslifespeaks.com/programs

www.ingramcontent.com/pod-product-compliance
Lightning Source LLC
Chambersburg PA
CBHW070923220526
45469CB00010B/1244